CaBullock

Flower Arrangements from Japan

KODANSHA INTERNATIONAL LTD.
Tokyo, New York and San Francisco

Flower Arrangements from Japan

by KASUMI TESHIGAWARA

with a Preface by SOFU TESHIGAWARA

photographs by MIKI TAKAGI

DISTRIBUTORS:

UNITED STATES: Harper & Row, Publishers, Inc.
10 East 53rd Street, New York, New York 10022

CANADA: Fitzhenry & Whiteside Limited
150 Lesmill Road, Don Mills, Ontario

CENTRAL AND SOUTH AMERICA: Feffer & Simons Inc.
31 Union Square, New York, New York 10003

BRITISH COMMONWEALTH (excluding Canada and the Far East): TABS
51 Weymouth Street, London W1

EUROPE: Boxerbooks Inc.
Limmatstrasse 111, 8031 Zurich

AUSTRALIA AND NEW ZEALAND: Paul Flesch & Co. Pty. Ltd.
259 Collins Street, Melbourne 3000

THAILAND: Central Department Store Ltd.
306 Silom Road, Bangkok

HONG KONG AND SINGAPORE: Books for Asia Ltd.
30 Tat Chee Avenue, Kowloon; 65 Crescent Road, Singapore 15

THE FAR EAST: Japan Publications Trading Company
P.O. Box 5030, Tokyo International, Tokyo

*Originally published in hardback under the title
Space and Color in Japanese Flower Arrangement.*

Published by Kodansha International Ltd., 2-12-21 Otowa,
Bunkyo-ku, Tokyo 112 and Kodansha International/USA, Ltd.,
10 East 53rd Street, New York, New York 10022 and 44 Montgomery
Street, San Francisco, California 94104. Copyright © in Japan
1974 by Kodansha International Ltd. All rights reserved.
Printed in Japan.

LCC 64-25790
ISBN 0-87011-238-4
JBC 5076-784586-2361

First edition, 1965
First paper edition, 1974

Table of Contents

Preface

THE SPIRIT OF IKEBANA
by Sofu Teshigawara

Ikebana has become so common even outside Japan that the word is likely to be overheard whenever flower-lovers gather around the world. The dissemination of ikebana abroad is indeed remarkable. The true student of this art, however, must understand from the outset that it is extremely important to appreciate ikebana as a nique art of Japan that was established and cultured in an old tradition. If it can be said that something discovered and developed in a country is most suitable there, ikebana is certainly one of the things most becoming to Japan.

In Japan, the conventional course hitherto has been to learn things from the West. In this sense, ikebana is the reverse and represents an unusual phenomenon, as Japan is the pioneer and many foreigners are now studying the art. This realization always prompts me to tell my students that they should be more progressive in their endeavors to master the art; they should not depend solely on the old and traditional, but attempt new and creative ideas to elevate the level of ikebana. To be founded on tradition in the true sense, I feel, should mean to make progress —not to remain at a standstill.

As my students know, I also frequently compare the nude art developed in Greece with the flower art of Japan. While these two arts may seem entirely different, they are basically similar to a remarkable degree. The physical beauty of the human body can be assessed in the same sense as the physical beauty of the flower. Because both are found endlessly various in structure and form, each is capable of an infinite variety of moods. Thus in each case one is faced with a fascinating range of artistic decisions to be made; the attitude of the sculptor expressing artistically the human body is in common with our efforts at arranging flowers artistically. This, in a sense, is ikebana, and I feel that it will prove an important point for those who would grasp the crux of this art.

There are many beautiful things on this earth of ours. It is equally true, however, that we are vulnerable to any number of things that can cause unpleasantness. It has always been my sincere desire that this beautiful art of ikebana will draw people closer together and enable them to maintain affection toward each other, and that this art will contribute to the peace and beautification of the world.

Introduction

On my several trips to Europe and the U.S.A., I found that there was a strong need for an up-to-date and easy-to-follow book on ikebana. There are a number of books in English and other foreign languages, and while some are beautifully illustrated, they seem to lack practical explanations of how to create the arrangements shown. Others fail to list substitutes readily available outside Japan.

Twelve years have passed since I started my own "Kasumi Class," and I have always hoped to do a practical guidebook for Westerners based on my teaching experience in the special class. Kodansha International has provided me with this golden opportunity; I have planned carefully and created new arrangements specifically for this book.

Basic techniques are explained in detail to provide the beginner a start in this fascinating art. By following the instructions on how to arrange the basic styles (pages 114-127) and by their repeated practice, proficiency can be obtained which will allow advancement to the more difficult freestyle arrangements. Arrangements suitable for special occasions such as Christmas, New Year, weddings, etc. are provided to make the book interesting also to the person who has already had some instruction in ikebana. Both classical and modern touches have been included in an effort to satisfy a broad range of individual tastes; substitute materials for each composition are listed with the same objective in mind.

My aims will be realized if the beginner, by following this book, becomes interested in the art of ikebana and finds that flower arranging can be done rather simply. This in turn often leads to further study and practice, through which one can obtain a feeling for the traditional spirit of ikebana. Also, for the person who has mastered the basic techniques, I hope that the wide variety of compositions will provide further inspiration to better flower arrangement.

I express my sincere gratitude to Mrs. Ayako Saito, for her help in translating the text into English, Mr. Masakazu Kuwata for the superb artwork and design, Mr. Miki Takagi for the outstanding photographs, Miss Machiko Saneto and Miss Michiko Oshima for their general assistance in making this publication possible.

June, 1964   KASUMI TESHIGAWARA

The following symbols are used throughout the book:

○ **First principal branch or stem** (*shin*)
□ **Second principal branch or stem** (*soe*)
△ **Third principal branch or stem** (*hikae*)
⊤ **Assistant branches or stems** (*jūshi*)

For a complete explanation of these and other basic terms and techniques, please refer to "Basic Arrangements," page 114.

Party Arrangements

New Year's

January is often referred to as the "month of pine" in Japan, and during this month, pine is a common component in flower arrangement. The pine's evergreen needles are regarded as a symbol of youth and longevity, and it is used for festive decorations together with red and white flowers symbolizing happiness. Within the gay composition shown here there also abounds solemn hope and resolution for the new year.

MATERIALS: 1 dead branch or driftwood
              5 pine branches   ○
              7 ilexes   □ T
              17 chrysanthemums   △

CONTAINER: bronze *moribana* vessel on a stand

HOW TO ARRANGE: *1.* In a large arrangement like this, driftwood or a piece of deadwood is used to take the place of *kenzan.* Arrange the driftwood to form the framework of the composition. *2.* Nail the three top branches of pine on the driftwood. *3.* Slant the ilex branches out, to contrast with the vertical pine, and nail them to the driftwood. *4.* The two pine branches at the base are inserted between the driftwood, top pine branches, and ilex. These do not have to be nailed. *5.* Remove all leaves from the chrysanthemums except five or six near the flower. Place the stems to the right in the spaces between the other branches.

SUBSTITUTES: Pine and driftwood are a must for New Year's, but when big pine branches are not available, increase the amount of driftwood without using tall pine. *Driftwood:* Use three to five bamboo. The green bamboo also acts as a substitute for pine in this case. *Ilex:* nandin, a plum, or vine. *Chrysanthemum:* lily. *Pine at base:* euonymus or boxwood.

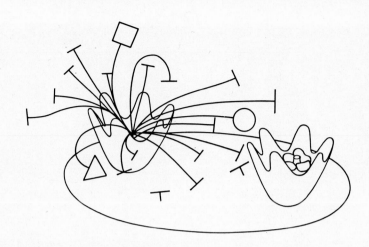

Valentine Day: Moonlight

Nature has provided plants with beautiful colors, lovely shapes and graceful lines, but it is for the arranger to create rhythm and movement. Since the mirror reflects not only the image of the composition, but also its surroundings, there must be harmony in color between the arrangement and the setting. As the observer moves, the reflection of the mirror also moves and one finds in it objects of nature such as the waterside and the soft breeze that sways the flowers.

MATERIALS: 7 acacias ○ □ T
             5 camellias △ T
            10 sweet peas T

CONTAINER: 2 glass vases
            1 wall mirror

HOW TO ARRANGE: *1.* Arrange acacia stems in the container so that their flowers can be observed from any direction. *2.* To add depth to the yellow of the acacias, arrange long and short stems of sweet peas around and in between the acacias. *3.* To shape the camellias, remove all the leaves except those nearest the flowers. Place one camellia in the center and another on the left side of the container. *4.* In the other container filled with water, float the most beautiful camellia blossom. *5.* Place two camellia flowers directly on the mirror so that it seems to reflect the image of the blossoms in the containers.

NOTE: Avoid the use of *kenzan* in a transparent glass container. Bend the stems in order to secure them firmly in the container.

SUBSTITUTES: Since the focus of this arrangement is in the composition of color, any yellow flower can be used to bring out this effect. *Floating camellia:* It is difficult to find any flower other than camellia that can stay fresh on the mirror without water for two days. Red roses can be used when floated on water.

From the plant world come lines of infinite beauty.
Here, peach branches are arranged in harmony
with the graceful lines of willow branches. Only
bright-colored flowers are used, so that the
warmth and gaiety of the season will be expressed
in every part of the composition.

MATERIALS: 2 willow branches ○ T
9 peach branches □ T
11 tulips △ T
7 snapdragons T

CONTAINER: straw hat with a small container in
the bottom

HOW TO ARRANGE: *1.* Cut willow branches in
different lengths so that the tips of the branches
will not be of the same length. Place the branches
firmly in the *kenzan* so that the composition will
not lose its shape when other materials are added;
this will also facilitate placement of other flowers
in the *kenzan*. *2.* Bend the peach branches
gently by holding each stem firmly in both hands
between the flowers. Place the stems in the
kenzan. *3.* Arrange tulips and snapdragons at
the base, with the taller stems in the center and to
the front to express overflowing strength. Shorter
stems are added in between.

SUBSTITUTES: *Branches:* (Scotch) broom, plum,
cherry, lilac, euonymus, cercis, anthurium. *Flowers:* gladiolus, freesia, narcissus, rose, iris, stock,
sultan.

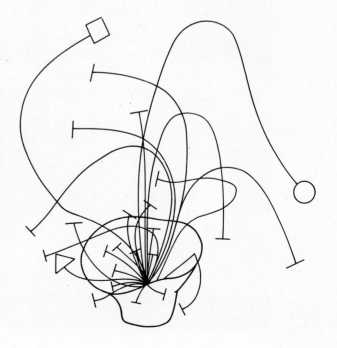

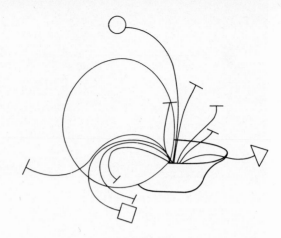

Wedding: Summer's Dream

This arrangement was made to be displayed where people were assembling to observe an event of utmost happiness and highest hopes. If the environment were not defined as such, however, the impression of the flowers would differ considerably. If the arrangement were to be displayed on a traditional tokonoma (alcove), no matter how bold and powerful the colors and forms might be, the arrangement would be similar to a framed picture which could be observed separately on its own virtues. Therefore, the soft harmony of the arrangement should be preserved to express effectively and contribute to the atmoshpere of the day, and should be portable so it can be displayed on the table, piano, or shelf, whichever seems most suitable.

MATERIALS: 1 marine plant of the coral family
5 asparagus ferns   ○ □ T
5 orchids   △ T

CONTAINER: glass vase

HOW TO ARRANGE: *1.*   Put a *kenzan* in the container and place in it the marine plant; the latter should rest against the back of the container to form a backdrop. This placement decides the shape of the arrangement.   *2.*   Have the fern dyed light blue. Intertwine the stems as you arrange them.   *3.*   Place the orchids between the ferns, keeping the lines of the flowers in harmony with those of the fern.   *4.*   Remember not to hide the "backdrop" marine plant.   *5.*   Cover the *kenzan* with white sand or pebbles.

SUBSTITUTES: *Marine plant:* asparagus fern or any other soft stems for outline. *Fern:* long vines or thin, painted-white branches to produce long lines. *Flower:* calla, lily, white carnation, white sweet pea for purity.

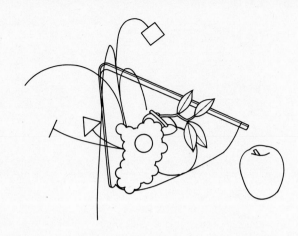

THANKSGIVING: RIPENING

In Japanese flower arrangement, there is the practice of coordinating natural objects and flowers throughout the year. Here, the focal point is in the cluster of grapes. The addition of other flowers and fruits that harmonize in color with the grapes gives richness to the arrangement. The cymbidium at the back provides a natural atmosphere to the whole composition.

MATERIALS: 2 clusters of grapes   ○
                      2 cymbidiums   □
                      2 orchids   △ T
                      2 Japanese "sampo" oranges (with stem and leaves)
                      1 apple

CONTAINER: bamboo basket

HOW TO ARRANGE: 1. The focal point must first be determined. In this case, it is in the center of the basket. 2. Place one bunch of grapes in line with the basket. Then place the other bunch gently on top of the first, thus creating the impression of one big cluster. 3. Wash the roots of the cymbidium and place them upright in the grape cluster, hiding the roots as much as possible. 4. Place the two oranges to the right so that they help to cover the base of the cymbidium. 5. Place one orchid between the grapes and the cymbidium, and the other orchid horizontally in the cluster of grapes from the left, with the stem touching the edge of the basket. 6. Complete the arrangement by adding an apple, away from the basket to the right. This placement helps to create a wider perspective.

NOTE: In this arrangement the position of the container is very important.

SUBSTITUTES: *Plant:* a small branch of pine, plum, hardy orange, or marine plant of the coral family. *Fruits:* green pepper, tomato, lemon, strawberry, cherry, apricot, or chestnut. *Flower:* other species of orchid, anthurium, or strelitzia.

20

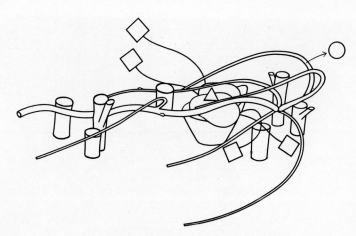

CHRISTMAS: SOFT GLOW

The bold lines of the mulberry branch add much gaiety to this large composition. The short pieces of birch trunk placed here and there, as if to block the flowing lines of the long mulberry branch, is another material that adds purity in harmony with the arrangement. The basic Christmas colors are seen in the container—carnations and holly.

MATERIALS: 1 drooping mulberry branch ○
           4 holly □
          12 white carnations △
          8 red carnations △
          7 pieces of white birch (about 4 inches in diameter):
                2 ten-inch pieces
                1 eight-inch piece
                2 six-inch pieces
                2 four-inch pieces

CONTAINER: glass bowl

HOW TO ARRANGE: *1.* Decide the placement of the container first, and rest the mulberry branch on it horizontally. *2.* Put the two six-inch birch stems as supports at the two places where the mulberry stem branches out. These rests help maintain the best angle of the mulberry branch. *3.* Place two birch stems around the the container to add thickness and depth to the arrangement. Then three pieces of birch are placed on the left to enhance the lines of the mulberry branch. *4.* Trim most of the tiny branches from the holly to reveal its lines, then place the stems in back and in front of the container. *5.* Tie the carnations into two bundles and place them in the center of the container with the white in the front and the red in the rear.

SUBSTITUTES: *Mulberry:* hardy orange. *White birch:* dead tree or driftwood, roots of trees, or stones. *Holly:* fir branches, or pine. *Carnations:* any red and white flowers.

Spring Arrangements

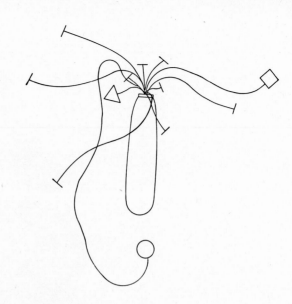

A Visit

Once there lived in Japan a great Buddhist priest who went on a pilgrimage all over the country. At homes where he had been offered lodging, he left behind hand-carved statuettes of Buddha. The simple, reassuring beauty of the sculpture influenced this floral creation.

Flowers are often arranged in harmony with a painting, calligraphy, or some other ornament in the background. These are not considered as a part of the materials for the floral composition but as altogether separate items. When viewed together, however, one often finds that they complement one another.

MATERIALS: 1 wisteria vine   ○
                5 Thunberg spirea   □ T
                6 freesia   △ T
CONTAINER: bamboo basket

HOW TO ARRANGE: *1.* First, bend the wisteria vine to create the desired line, then place it in the container. *2.* Since spirea branches cannot be bent, reveal their graceful lines by removing unnecessary twigs. Place the branches like outstretched arms, being careful, however, to avoid balancing them equally on both sides of the container. *3.* Remove leaves from the freesia and scatter them appropriately between the spirea. Before placing the flowers in the container, crush the base of the stems so that the flowers will face various angles instead of sitting upright.

SUBSTITUTES: *Foliage:* cercis, Japanese red plum, clematis, stauntonia, Boston ivy, bine, or any branch that hangs down. *Flowers:* carnation, chrysanthemum, rose, California poppy, rodgersia, sweet pea, or any small, gentle flower.

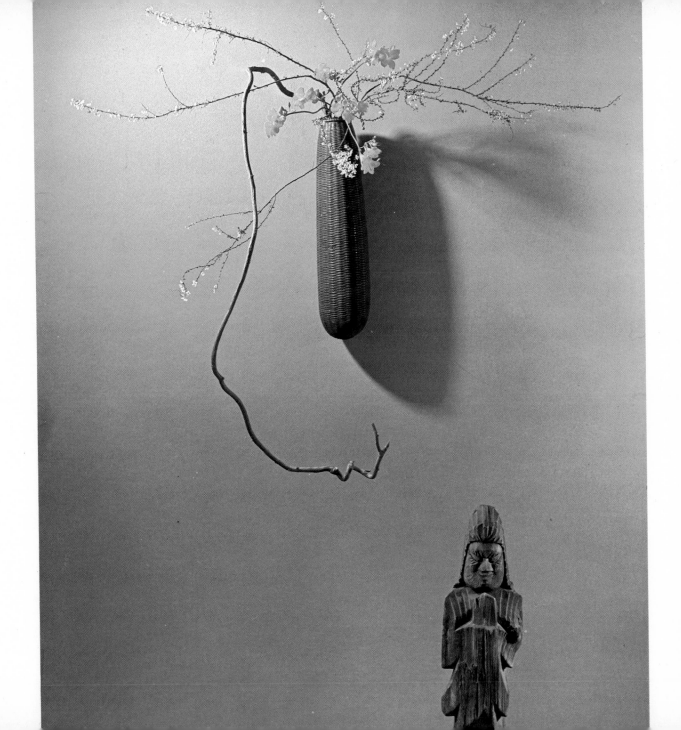

Although the Doll Festival is not one of the most important celebrations in Japan, it is welcomed as a harbinger of spring. The lovely peach blossoms contribute gaily to the cheerful mood of the season. Here, the peach blends well with the yellow of the freesia. For years the combination of pink and yellow has been used in Japanese flower arrangement.

MATERIALS: 2 peach branches ○ □

             4 cumquat (Japanese citrus) branches △ T

           10 freesias   T

CONTAINER: glass vase

HOW TO ARRANGE: *1.* Remove all leaves from cumquat branches and put all four branches in the container as illustrated. They are held in place by the other materials that are later placed between these branches. *2.* Place peach branches upright firmly between the cumquat branches. *3.* Remove leaves from freesia stems and insert flowers in a bunch at the base of the branches.

NOTE: For this type of arrangement, a small-mouth vase is preferable.

SUBSTITUTES: *Foliage:* plum, cherry, pine, redbuds, spindle tree, Thunberg spirea, forsythia, pine, or any branch possessing straight lines. *Flowers:* carnation, narcissus, or other flowers that harmonize with the branch materials.

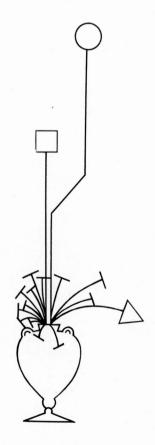

INVITATION

The center of interest of this composition lies in
the dark yellow vase in the middle, with the
curving lines of the branches that seem to be
enclosing the space on both sides. The beauty
of the arrangement is created by the curving
lines and the placement of flowers and tiny
branches at the mouth of the container. The
gentle rhythm of the tiny leaves and flowers have
a way of merging into the feelings of the observer.

MATERIALS: 6 euonymuses (spindle-tree) ○ □ T

       5 epidendrons   △ T

CONTAINER: *nage-ire* ceramic vase

HOW TO ARRANGE: *1.* Branches are held in
place by bending. *2.* Place long branches of
euonymus to the left and right of the container.
Place the third branch to the right of center.
3. Place epidendrons beginning with the center
ones first. *4.* Complete the arrangement by
placing shorter branches of euonymus near the
mouth of the container to cover the base of
the branches.

SUBSTITUTES: *Foliage:* Thunberg spirea, pussy
willow, broom, kerria, celastrus, plum, cherry.
Flowers: carnation, rose, hydrangea, clematis,
chrysanthemum, narcissus, lily.

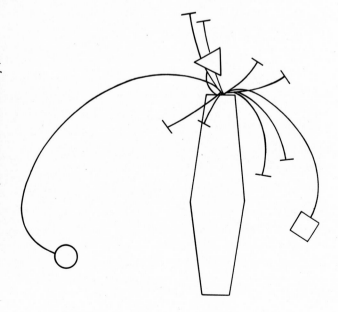

The traditional Japanese phrase "one flower and one leaf" does not necessarily mean that only one blossom and a single leaf are used in an arrangement. It refers to a composition in which materials have been reduced to the minimum. Simplicity is the keynote in Japanese literature, sculpture, painting, tea ceremony, noh, and other fields of culture. In ikebana too, one finds special joy in creating a very simple arrangement such as this.

MATERIALS: 1 eucalyptus ○
　　　　　　 1 camellia △

CONTAINER: black-banded, unglazed ceramic vessel

HOW TO ARRANGE: *1.* Place a small *kenzan* in the container. *2.* Cut most of the branches from the eucalyptus, leaving only those at the top. Remove some of the branches at the top to leave more weight on either the left or the right side. *3.* Place the eucalyptus upright in the *kenzan*. *4.* Remove leaves from the camellia, leaving only those near the flower that add to its motion or rhythm. Place the camellia at the base.

SUBSTITUTES: *Foliage:* spirea, pine, acacia. *Flower:* rose, chrysanthemum, dahlia, herbaceous peony, clematis, sunflower, anthurium, tree peony.

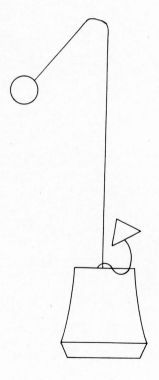

Waiting for Spring

Can you visualize a country fireplace with people sitting around it, waiting for spring to come? This arrangement was made with such a scene in mind.

When using a container with a distinctive design such as this piece of folkcraft, it is best to keep its surface exposed as much as possible.

MATERIALS: 6 Thunberg spirea ○ □ T
2 clivia (Kafir lily) △

CONTAINER: blue and white Spanish dish

HOW TO ARRANGE: *1.* Since Thunberg spirea stems are very thin, wrap their bases with tissue paper before placing them on the *kenzan*. Also remember to cut the stems underwater. *2.* Place two Thunberg spirea stems (○ and □), one to the left and the other to the right of the container, making them spread out almost horizontally. *3.* Cut the stems of clivia very short and place them in the center. *4.* Place the remaining spirea stems as in the diagram. The length of these stems should be varied.

SUBSTITUTES: *Foliage:* broom, plum, forsythia, cercis, Japanese allspice, cherry, spindle tree. *Flowers:* amaryllis, anthurium, rose, iris, daffodil, gladiolus.

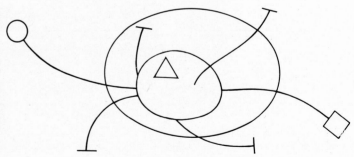

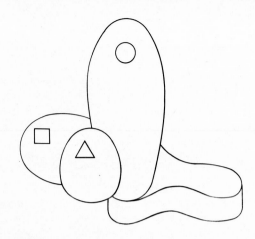

Spring Hill

Water is an ever-necessary element in expressing the spirit of any particular season. The water's edge, where flowers bloom and thickets cast shadows, affords us a place of relaxation in this complicated modern age. This arrangement consists of three masses by the water's edge.

The technique of grouping materials in mass form was created by the Sogetsu school after the end of the war. Different from the flowing lines of traditional Japanese flower arrangement, where primary attention is given to color and line, this kind of mass arrangement offers a feeling of weight and strength.

MATERIALS: 7 Japanese cypress branches   ○
            30 pink sweet peas   □
            30 yellow sweet peas   △
CONTAINER: lacquer vase
HOW TO ARRANGE: *1.* Make a mass with cypress branches by tying the stems firmly with florist wire. Place *kenzan* on the left side of the vase and insert the mass. *2.* Trim and shape the tops of the leafy branches and fill in empty spaces with small branches. *3.* Make two masses of sweet peas—the yellow one round and the pink one somewhat oblong. Insert the masses in the *kenzan*, the oblong one in the back and the round one in front.

NOTE: *1.* When creating a mass arrangement, it is always better to choose materials with an abundance of flowers and leaves. *2.* Since it is difficult to reshape the stems after they are tied in a mass, be sure to put the stems into shape before tying them.

SUBSTITUTES: *Foliage:* Japanese cedar, erica, spindle tree, boxwood, camellia. *Flowers:* gladiolus, rose, chrysanthemum, tulip, stock, lupine, narcissus, carnation.

TOWER OF FLOWERS

In traditional ikebana there were many rules, such as the number of stems and the shape of the arrangement, which had to be adhered to. Within the past thirty years, however, flower arrangement has gone through wonderful developments that now allow us to express our feelings almost freely in a floral composition. Anyone possessing inborn qualities of creation can master this art after learning the essential techniques required for free expression.

This arrangement was made for an Occidental setting.

MATERIALS: 16 gladioli ○

              8 sorbuses (mountain ash) □ △

CONTAINER: glass plate

HOW TO ARRANGE: *1.* After removing leaves and buds, wire the gladiolus flowers together, working gradually from the longest ones first. Place this bunch firmly in the *kenzan.* *2.* Wire sorbuses into two bunches and fix one at the upper part and one at the base of the gladioli.

SUBSTITUTES: *Flowers:* orchid, chrysanthemum, rose, canna, calla, dahlia, snapdragon, stock, narcissus, sweet pea, carnation, anthurium. *Sorbus:* acacia.

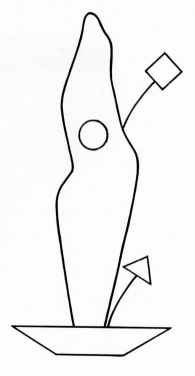

DUSK

This kind of table arrangement is most inviting for a cozy family get-together in the quiet hours of the evening. It also helps to stimulate pleasant dreams of tomorrow. The feeling of the arrangement can be either gay or quiet, depending upon the colors of the materials used.

MATERIALS: 7 stocks ○ T

30 white sweet peas ☐

30 purple sweet peas △ T

CONTAINER: shallow rectangular vase

HOW TO ARRANGE: *1.* Place one *kenzan* on the left side of the container and one on the right side. The water surface visible between the two *kenzan* is very effective. *2.* On the left *kenzan*, place the longest stem of stock first. Then arrange other stocks of different lengths as in the diagram. *3.* Make a mass with white sweet peas and place this in the center of the *kenzan*. *4.* Take half of the purple sweet peas and cut the stems a little shorter than the white ones. Wire them together and place the mass to the left of the white sweet peas. *5.* Make a mass with the remaining purple sweet peas and insert on the right *kenzan*.

SUBSTITUTES: Any combination of flowers: anthurium, narcissus, rose, freesia, gladiolus, iris, snapdragon, chrysanthemum.

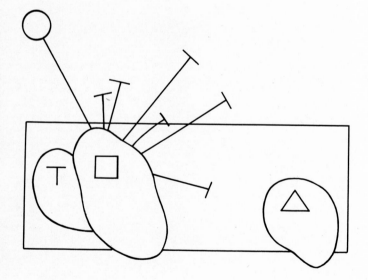

40

SWORD

An arrangement of Japanese iris symbolizes Boys' Festival held on May 5, when families pray for their boys to grow up strong, healthy, and noble. A certain dignity and manliness, reminiscent of the Japanese warrior (samurai) of olden days, is clearly expressed in this arrangement.

MATERIALS: 5 Japanese iris ○ □ △ T
12 iris leaves T
Handful of white gravel

CONTAINER: a pair of black, half-moon-shaped basins

HOW TO ARRANGE: *1.* Place a *kenzan* in each of the containers. *2.* Decide the position of flowers first. Place three flowers upright in the rear *kenzan* and two in the front, starting with the longest stem. *3.* The ends of the leaves are pointed and curved to one side. Group together two or three leaves with the points facing inward. *4.* Place a group of three leaves in front of the flowers so that the middle leaf will hide part of the flower stem. This improves the appearance. *5.* Place a group of two or three leaves in back of the flowers. In either case the leaves should be cut shorter than the flowers and placed close against the flower stem as if to touch it. Groups of leaves are placed in front and back of each flower. *6.* Cover the *kenzan* with gravel.

SUBSTITUTES: *Flower:* gladiolus. *Leaves:* iris, New Zealand flax.

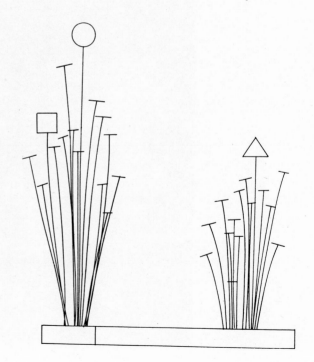

Summer Arrangements

CRIMSON MEMORIES

In an arrangement using a small container, with materials reduced to the absolute minimum, or in a composition where there is space allowance for more materials, the impression and imagination of the observer can be broadened and deepened.

MATERIALS: 1 epidendron ○
1 great reed □
2 bunches of grapes made of glass △ T

CONTAINER: glass bowl

HOW TO ARRANGE: *1.* Since *kenzan* should not be used in a transparent container, marbles etc. are used to hold the stems. Wire together two bunches of glass grapes. Let one bunch hang to the outside and one inside of the container. *2.* Cut the epidendron stem underwater and place it between the glass grapes. *3.* Cut the stem of the great reed underwater. Place it upright between the glass grapes and let one leaf hang over the middle of the grapes.

SUBSTITUTES: *Glass grapes:* Place marbles or small stones inside the container to take the place of a *kenzan*. *Reed and flower:* clematis, or rose, or thistle alone; two long-stem flowers and some short branches at the base.

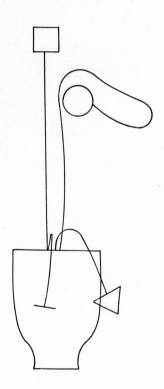

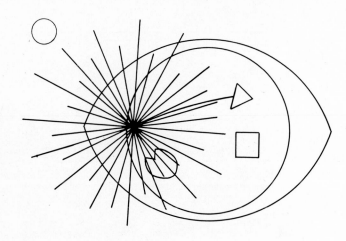

TROPICAL SUN

Here, our interest is centered in the distinctive container. The water in the vessel seems to reflect the glittering sun, and the flower looks refreshing in the heat. Water plays an important part in providing coolness in a tropical atmosphere.

MATERIALS: 1 ananas ○
            1 water lily □
            2 leaves of water lily △ T

CONTAINER: lacquer basin

HOW TO ARRANGE: *1.* Place one *kenzan* in the left side of the container and another small *kenzan* a little to the right of the center. *2.* Cut off ananas near the root and place it vertically on the left *kenzan*. *3.* Cut off the stem of one water-lily leaf and place it under the ananas to cover the *kenzan*. *4.* Cut the stem of the water lily very short and insert in the right *kenzan*. The length of the stem should be about the same height as that of the needles on the *kenzan*. The flower will then look as if it were floating. *5.* Take the other water-lily leaf and press its long stem between your fingers to soften it. This makes the leaf float better. Insert the end of the stem on the left *kenzan* under the ananas, and let the leaf float in the open water at the back of the water lily.

SUBSTITUTES: *Foliage:* anthurium leaves, spirea, calla leaves. *Note:* Select well-shaped branches and leaves that are attractive from any direction. *Flower:* camellia, peony, dahlia, clematis, rose, wild lily, chrysanthemum. *Note:* Two or three flowers can be floated without using *kenzan*. Do not use the leaves.

The stone used here is of a soft, porous quality that can easily be carved. When this is not available, a stone or stones of your choice can be used, behind which a water holder can be placed. Instead of one large stone, several small ones can be placed around a water container. The main point is to match the stone and the materials to produce a rustic beauty.

MATERIALS: 5 China roots ○ □ T
2 lilium (gold-banded lily) △ T

CONTAINER: hand-carved vessel of *oya-ishi* (soft, porous stone)

HOW TO ARRANGE: *1.* Place *kenzan* in the front part of the container. *2.* Since it is difficult to keep China root standing, it is better to make the branches as light as possible by removing unnecessary leaves, keeping only about ten. Cut the base of the stem in a slant and insert in *kenzan*. *3.* Remove leaves from the lilies, retaining only those that enhance the flowers in the arrangement. *4.* Since the stems of the lilies are thin and the flowers large, it is difficult to hold them in position. Place the stems in the center, resting them against the China root.

SUBSTITUTES: *Foliage:* wild rose, enkianthus, hardy orange, sprengeri. *Flowers:* clematis, canna, gladiolus, chrysanthemum, anthurium, rose, sunflower.

50

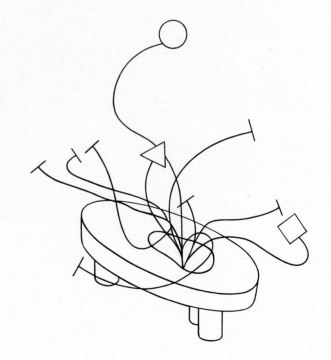

The beauty of the red roses is enhanced by the contrasting colors of the asparagus fern, the glass vase, and the marbles. Though strong in color, the rose petals are quick to weaken and lose shape, somewhat resembling a flickering flame. The soft line of the green asparagus fern is added to lend a helping hand.

MATERIALS: 5 red roses   □   △   T
             4 asparagus ferns   ○   T
             green marbles
             blue marbles

CONTAINER: glass *nage-ire* vase

HOW TO ARRANGE: *1.* These marbles have been selected because their color matches the shade of the container. Fill the container with green marbles to take the place of a *kenzan*. *2.* Cutting stems underwater, insert the stem of the longest rose about two inches into the marbles, tilting the blossom to the right. Place three roses together in the center. Place one rosebud to the right at the back. Leave one leaf between the blossoms at the top and one leaf near the mouth of the container. Remove all the other leaves. *3.* Place three asparagus ferns on the left side of the container, showing clearly the three flowing lines. Remove leaves from the stems of the ferns that go inside the container. Put one short asparagus stem in the right side.

SUBSTITUTES: *Flowers:* dahlia, anthurium, camellia. *Fern:* smilax.

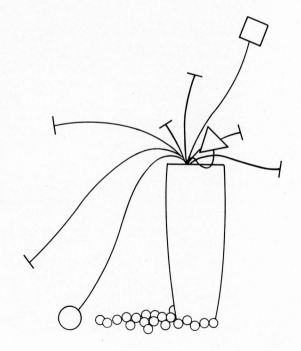

Movement

Arranged in their beautiful natural forms, some materials can give the impression of branches and flowers swaying in the wind. The same materials, however, depending on the method of arrangement or the container used, display effects completely halting such movements. In this arrangement, motion has been added artificially to the otherwise still composition.

MATERIALS: 17 scirpus ○ T

6 calla △ T

CONTAINER: glass fruit dish

HOW TO ARRANGE: *1.* Place a *kenzan* in the center of the container. *2.* Hold the scirpus at different lengths and bend the stems lightly with the fingers. Then line them up as you would draw lines on paper. Bunch the stems tightly together—up to about four inches from the *kenzan*, and insert them in the *kenzan*. Start with the longer ones in the back and then the shorter ones in front. Several short ones can be placed in between the longer stems at the back. *3.* Arrange the calla at the base of the scirpus, with the tips of the flowers pointing in the direction of the scirpus ends. The calla lilies at the base enhance the lines of the scirpus.

SUBSTITUTES: *Scirpus:* scouring rush, wheat, New Zealand flax. *Flowers:* anthurium, iris, strelitzia, dahlia, sunflower (depending on the color of the container).

54

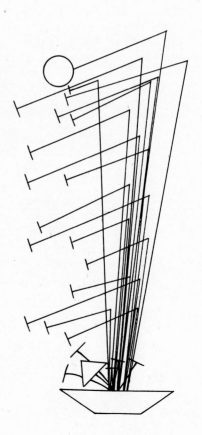

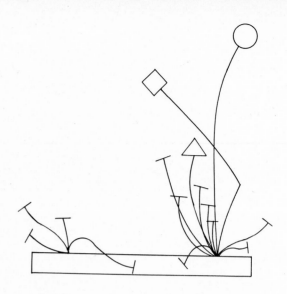

RIVERSIDE

This low and expansive composition shows the water surface between the plants, suggesting a beautiful landscape between mountains. The point of interest is in the use of the water surface, not as sustenance for plants as is done ordinarily, but as an object to be observed.

MATERIALS: 8 Thunberg spirea ○ □ T
5 candock leaves △ T
2 candock flowers T

CONTAINER: unglazed ceramic basin

HOW TO ARRANGE: *1.* Place one *kenzan* in the right side of the container and one in the left. *2.* Select two Thunberg spirea branches about the length of the container and place in the right *kenzan.* These branches determine the lines of the finished arrangement. *Note:* When spirea branches are so shaped that they look better in the left side, then the left *kenzan* should be used. *3.* Soak a cigarette in water. With a flower pump, insert the brownish liquid into the candock stems from the cut end at the base. Preserving the stems in this way will prevent the leaves from curling. *4.* Place two leaves with long stems near the base of the spirea branches. Then arrange three short leaves around from the back to the front at the base. This helps to cover the *kenzan.* *5.* Place two rather short flowers between the leaves. *6.* Finish by placing a short, thick, leafy branch of spirea in the left *kenzan* to give the arrangement breadth and balance.

SUBSTITUTES: *Foliage:* Scotch broom, kerria, azalea (or any material with small leaves). *Leaf and flower:* calla, clematis, waterlily, anthurium.

In Japan, as elsewhere, there can be found settings that make the most of the simple and unsophisticated qualities of things in everyday life. The container used here is a simple and familiar bamboo shade that one usually hangs by the window to bring coolness to the house. The materials chosen are also readily found in a corner of one's garden or along a mountain path.

MATERIALS:　2 scirpus　　○ □
　　　　　　　1 thistle　　△
　　　　　　　1 caladium　T

CONTAINER:　homemade vase (empty can wrapped with a bamboo shade)

HOW TO ARRANGE:　*1.* *Kenzan* are not used in this tall-vase arrangement. Cut stems of the scirpus in different lengths and place in the container. *2.* Remove all leaves from the thistle except one at the top. Let the leaf hang over the mouth of the container. *3.* Press the stem of the caladium between the fingers gently. Insert it between the stems of scirpus and thistle. The tip of the leaf should point upward.

NOTE:　Be sure to cut all of the stems underwater.

SUBSTITUTES:　*Stems:* thin branches of spirea, weeping willow (tips of branches will hang down in this case). *Flower and leaf:* 1 chrysanthemum, 2 or 3 pinks, 1 clematis.

58

Summer in the Alps

This is a creation from my reminiscence of a moment on a Swiss mountainside, where the flowers, rocks, and clear air seemed like those of another world. Cactus is used here to create the feeling of mountain coolness.

MATERIALS: 3 cacti   ○ □ T
2 sunflowers   △ T

CONTAINER: red-and-black-striped ceramic bowl

HOW TO ARRANGE: *1.* Place two *kenzan* alongside of each other. *2.* Insert the longest cactus in the center. *3.* Cut the other two cacti shorter than the first. Insert them a little to the front of the first, the shortest one on the left, and the other on the right. *4.* Remove all leaves from the sunflowers. Insert the taller one in front of the first cactus. *5.* Place the shorter sunflower in front to hide the stem of the other one.

SUBSTITUTES: *Foliage:* aspidistra, rubber, New Zealand flax, monstera. *Flowers:* cosmos, dahlia, clematis, calla, anthurium, strelitzia.

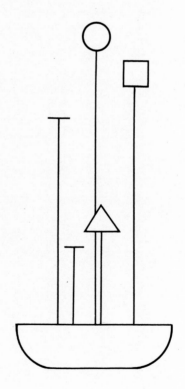

Fall Arrangements

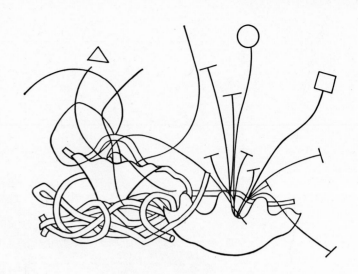

A Tale of the Sea

The sea provides us with an abundance of stories, songs, and colors. To us the sea has a variety of meanings, and sometimes it brings back pleasant memories of days spent by the seaside. It also gives full play to our imagination and unfolds in our minds a world unknown.

MATERIALS: 5 wisteria vines
5 gladioli ○ □ T
8 celastrus △ T
4 plume poppies T

CONTAINERS: 1 shell
1 glass bowl

HOW TO ARRANGE: *1.* Rest the wisteria vine on the edge of the shell to determine its appropriate height. To the left of the shell, nail the vines together to form a stand for the glass bowl. *2.* Put a *kenzan* in each of the containers. *3.* Place in the shell the longest gladiolus. Add the others in the shape of an open fan. *4.* Arrange plume poppies together at the base of the gladioli. *5.* In the glass bowl, arrange the celastrus by intertwining its branches. Long stems of celastrus are placed extending to the right to combine the two materials. One stem is placed to the far left to contrast with the long stem to the right. *6.* To complete the arrangement, place one celastrus in the shell to connect the two containers.

SUBSTITUTES: *Flowers:* canna, strelitzia, cosmos. *Celastrus:* hardy orange, wild rose. *Plume poppy:* pampas grass.

The autumnal color of boxwood harmonizes well with the roses on the surface of the water. In contrast to the cold appearance of the basins, the warm color of the boxwood and roses brings an atmosphere of peaceful autumn from the countryside into the home.

MATERIALS: 2 boxwood branches ○ □ T
2 roses △ T

CONTAINER: 2 half-moon-shaped black basins

HOW TO ARRANGE: *1.* Place one *kenzan* in each of the two containers a little off center. On the rear *kenzan* place one long branch of boxwood horizontally to the front, with the branch almost touching the water surface. The tip of the branch extends to the front of the container. *2.* In the front *kenzan* insert the shorter branch of box-wood. Finally, arrange short thick branches at the base to cover the *kenzan*. Both *kenzan* should be covered so that they cannot be seen from any direction. *3.* Cut stems from the roses and float the flowers near each *kenzan*.

SUBSTITUTES: *Foliage:* euonymus, Japanese cypress, cryptomeria, Japanese red plum. *Flower:* chrysanthemum.

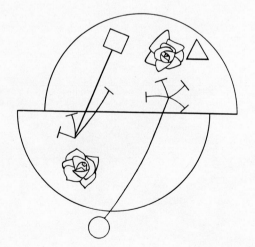

CRIMSON THREAD

The image of a beautiful sunset is portrayed here
by flaming red maple leaves that seem to be born
from the setting sun, and the matching red container amplifies the theme. The deep purplish
blue of the iris resembles the evening shadows
that begin to fall around this time of day.

MATERIALS: 4 maple branches ○ □ T
　　　　　　3 irises △ T

CONTAINER: vermilion *nage-ire* ceramic vase

HOW TO ARRANGE: *1.* The stem of the vertical
maple branch is made to touch the bottom of the
container. *2.* The other two long maple branches
are placed so as to rest against the mouth of the
container. *3.* Crush the base of the iris stems
with your fingers. Flowers are placed in the
container so that they face the viewer. Insert the
first iris to the right, the second flower to the
front, and the third iris to the back. *4.* Insert a
short branch of maple leaves in the center at the
base to establish the focal point.

SUBSTITUTES: *Foliage:* spindle tree (whose leaves
have turned yellow), euonymus alata, red Japanese
plum. *Flowers:* chrysanthemum, carnation.

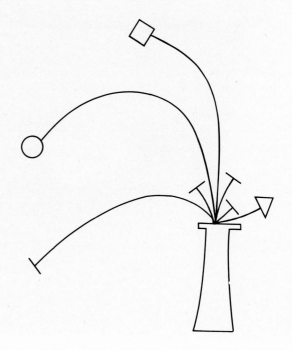

The Advent of Autumn

Autumn is perhaps the most beautiful of all seasons, when we are awed by the spaciousness of nature. The sky is so clear that we can identify in the sunlight each fluttering bird and each falling leaf.

MATERIALS: 4 pomegranate branches ○ □ T
4 gerberas △ T

CONTAINER: twin ceramic pot

HOW TO ARRANGE: *1.* Remove all leaves from the pomegranate branches. In the left orifice of the container place one long pomegranate branch extending to the left. Branch 2 is placed in the same orifice, slanting horizontally to the right, and is kept lower than the left branch. *2.* Assistant branches 3 and 4 are placed in the same opening. The secret of this arrangement lies in keeping the branches low and spread out on both sides of the container. *3.* In the right orifice, place the longest gerbera, making the flower seem to reach out to the pomegranate on the left. Insert three gerberas in the same side, arranging their flowers near the mouth of the pot.

SUBSTITUTES: *Foliage:* persimmon, chestnut, mandarin orange. *Flowers:* rose, carnation, chrysanthemum.

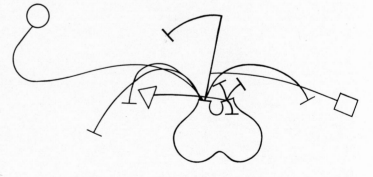

The spirit of traditional Japanese flower arrangement is retained in the simplicity of this composition. The use of bright colors has been avoided in both materials and container to create an image of the ancient capital.

MATERIALS: 2 branches of cactus ○ □ T
2 chrysanthemums △ T

CONTAINER: double-mouthed *nage-ire* ceramic vessel

HOW TO ARRANGE: *1.* Place one long cactus branch leaning out from and over the right-hand opening of the container. About four inches of the stem should be inside the container. *2.* Place the shorter cactus horizontally to the left from the same opening. *3.* Remove all the leaves of the chrysanthemum stems except one or two good ones near the flowers. Place the longer stem first. The shorter one should be just long enough for the flower to cover the base of the stems near the mouth of the container. Chrysanthemums are also placed in the right-hand opening.

SUBSTITUTES: *Foliage:* red Japanese plum, enkianthus. *Flowers:* lily, gentian.

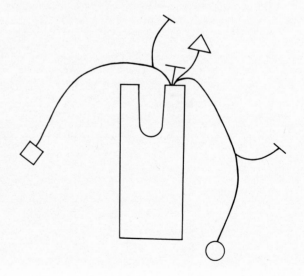

A Clown and His Horse

Through the rhythm created by the plants, this composition was arranged with the hope of expressing the mood of a horse and its comical master. The materials were chosen to make the most of the unique vessel.

MATERIALS: 3 anthuriums ○ □ △

　　　　　　 15 Japanese cypress branches T

CONTAINER: fancy ceramic vase

HOW TO ARRANGE: *1.* When containers of peculiar shape are used, *kenzan* cannot be held in place. Dense foliage, such as the cypress used here, should be placed in the container first to function as *kenzan*. *2.* Wire two anthuriums together at the base and insert in the right side of the container. *3.* One short anthurium is inserted in the left with its yellowish spadix facing upward.

SUBSTITUTES: *Flowers:* strelitzia, carnation, calla, lily. *Foliage:* cryptomeria, boxwood, maple.

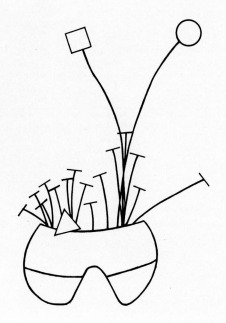

74

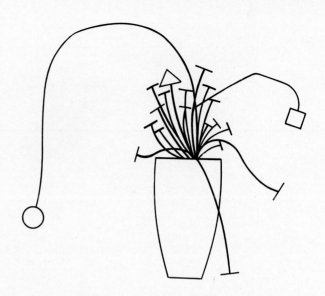

AUTUMN LIGHT

One distinctive feature of Japanese flower arrangement is the use of only that part of the branch that brings out the particular characteristic of the plant. All the other twigs are eliminated. Here, you can see that more than half of the leaves, twigs, and fruits have been cut from the branches. Tradition has it that pomegranate fruits are children of God. The lustrous red of the fruit that shines in the sunlight resembles the purity of children's rosy cheeks and lips. Deep blue flowers are combined here to enhance the beautiful red and yellow of the fruit.

MATERIALS: 3 pomegranate branches ○ □ T
16 gentian △ T
CONTAINER: large ceramic vase
HOW TO ARRANGE: *1.* Do not use a *kenzan.*

When making a *nage-ire* arrangement of branches bearing heavy pieces of fruit, place a cross support in the mouth of the vase. Tie the longest pomegranate branch to the cross-bar support. *2.* Place the other two branches by leaning them against the cross support. *3.* Insert gentian stems between the cross support and the pomegranate branches, beginning with the longest stem and placing the flowers toward the right side of the container. Complete the arrangement by placing the shortest gentian to the left at the mouth of the container.

SUBSTITUTES: *Foliage:* persimmon, apple, chestnut, mandarin orange. *Flowers:* chrysanthemum, iris.

76

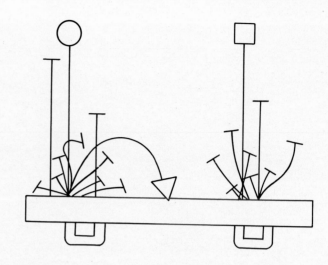

DREAM

This arrangement was created to picture some of the natural objects that are gradually disappearing from urban life: the soft sound of a chestnut falling on the roof; the sound of rustling leaves at dusk; the clear skies on days of bright sunlight and on starlit nights.

MATERIALS: 5 fothers ○ □ T
6 anthuriums △ T
9 patrinias T

CONTAINER: oblong modern container

HOW TO ARRANGE: *1.* Place one *kenzan* to the left and one to the right of center in the container. Trim leaves from the fothers. Place three fothers of different lengths upright in the left *kenzan* and two in the right *kenzan*. *2.* When arranging anthuriums, the shades of the flowers and the curves of the stems should be considered. They are placed in front of the fothers. *3.* One long anthurium is placed in the left *kenzan* with its flower bending toward the center of the container. Another long stem is placed in the right *kenzan*. *4.* Three short anthuriums are placed together in the left *kenzan*. Finally, one small anthurium is placed low in the right *kenzan* with its flower facing the front. *5.* Remove all leaves from the patrinias and place the stems together at the base of the anthuriums in the left *kenzan*. Complete the arrangement by placing patrinias in the right *kenzan*. Their stems should be a little taller than those on the left, and their flowers should fill the space between the two anthuriums.

SUBSTITUTES: *Fother:* pampas grass, foxtail, cattail. *Anthurium:* rose, strelitzia, gladiolus. *Patrinia:* gypsophila, evening mist.

Even a casual glance around us reveals that plants exist in almost every conceivable form. However, we find that no matter how extremely opposite their characteristics, those differing plants seem to possess similarity in some respects. It is amazing to notice that even when contrasting materials are arranged, there is perfect harmony in the composition.

MATERIALS: 12 New Zealand flax ○ □ T
15 celastrus △ T

CONTAINER: long modern basin

HOW TO ARRANGE: *1.* Place two pairs of *kenzan* in the container, leaving between the pairs a space equal to the size of one *kenzan*. *2.* Use the New Zealand flax in order of height, inserting the tallest in the center of the right-hand *kenzan*; arrange shorter ones in front, back, and between the tall flax. *3.* In the center of the left *kenzan* insert the thickest, straightest stem of celastrus and intertwine the other vines as you arrange them. *4.* Extend the celastrus vines to the right, in front and back of the New Zealand flax. This extension unites the two plants of different lines to form one composition.

NOTE: This is a combination of lines in green monochrome.

SUBSTITUTES: *Curved lines:* balloon vine, stauntonia. *Straight lines:* aspidistra, pampas (for contrasting color combination).

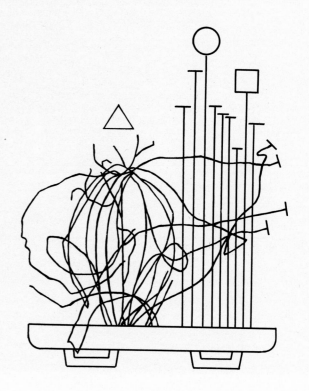

Winter Arrangements

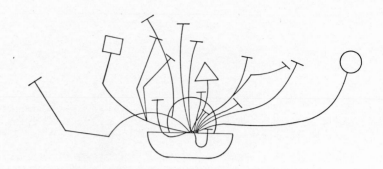

SOBRIETY

The dignified form of the moss-covered plum branches and the gold bands of the vessel harmonize beautifully in subduing the three different shades of red. In Japan, a new flower arrangement is always considered a gesture of welcome. Discretion and austerity are called for in such compositions.

MATERIALS: 5 moss-covered plum branches

○ □ T

4 strelitzias △

7 plum branches T

13 nandin berry branches T

CONTAINER: large red water-basin

HOW TO ARRANGE: *1.* Place a *kenzan* in the center of the container. *2.* Arrange two moss-covered plum branches so that one projects to the left and one to the right of the container, nailing them together at the point of intersection for stability. Nail the other three branches to the first two main branches. *3.* Place five thin plum branches in the *kenzan*, leaving two thin branches until the last. *4.* Arrange the strelitzias to the right, placing the longer ones first. *5.* Place the nandin branches in one mass in the front, being careful not to let them droop. *6.* Complete the arrangement by placing two plum branches in the front.

NOTE: Tips of all branches should face upward.

SUBSTITUTES: *Foliage:* cherry, spirea, magnolia, pussy willow, vaccinium, Japanese red plum. *Flower:* chrysanthemum, narcissus, carnation, rose, iris, lily, gentian, gladiolus. *Berries:* sorbus, pampas grass, Japanese pampas, miscanthus, China root.

84

INACTIVITY AND MOTION

This composition does not show the natural lines
of the materials, but treats them in mass form.
When viewing this arrangement, one of course
sees that it is motionless, and yet it gives the impression that it may begin to move any minute,
or is moving, or has been in motion.

MATERIALS: 10 cryptomeria branches ○

7 carnations △

CONTAINER: ceramic compote

HOW TO ARRANGE: 1. Place *kenzan* in the container. 2. Wire together thick cryptomeria
branches to form a mass and place it upright in
the *kenzan*. 3. Place carnations in front of the
cryptomeria, using the shortest one at the base.
The length of the flowers should be slightly
varied. 4. After placing all of the carnations,
decide the general form of the arrangement and
then trim the cryptomeria to the desired shape.

NOTE: In working with mass form like this,
always draw a sketch of the shape you want to
create before deciding the materials.

SUBSTITUTES: *Foliage:* Japanese cypress, azalea,
boxwood, euonymus, camellia leaves, gypsophila, upright. *Flowers:* rose, narcissus, tulip,
camellia, chrysanthemum, dahlia, gladiolus.

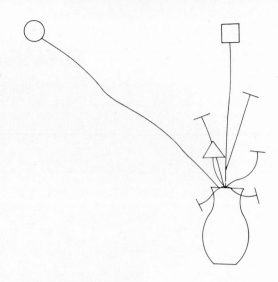

TRANQUILITY

The title of this arrangement comes from the atmosphere created by the vase, the space formed by the branches, and the color harmony of the composition and its background. The first thing one notices in a flower arrangement is the color, and next, its form. Even with the same materials, the atmosphere of compositions may vary to any extent, and their distinct qualities are brought out and greatly influenced by the environment, such as the furnishings of a room, or at times by the feeling that comes from the container.

MATERIALS: 2 Japanese red-plum branches ○ T
              3 ilexes □ T
              2 yellow roses △ T

CONTAINER: earthenware vase

HOW TO ARRANGE: *1.* Since this is a *nage-ire* container, branches are held in place by bending. Place the longest branch of Japanese red plum in the container, allowing it to extend out to the left. *2.* Next place the longest branch of ilex so that it is almost vertical. (The mouth of the container will now be fairly congested.) *3.* One dense, short fill-in branch of Japanese plum is placed in the front. *4.* Place the two shorter branches of ilex, one in front and the other at the back of the vertical branch. *5.* Remove unnecessary leaves from the roses and complete the arrangement by placing the upper rose first, then the other at the base.

SUBSTITUTES: *Plum branches:* euonymus, plum, cherry spirea. *Ilex:* paulownia, nandin berries. *Rose:* chrysanthemum, iris, clematis, narcissus, stock, hydrangea, snapdragon, lily.

This composition presents an image of bright red flames in a fireplace, flickering high and low, and seeming to absorb all of the colors within and around.

MATERIALS: 70 foxtails, dyed red ○ □ T
40 small chrysanthemums △ T

CONTAINER: ceramic compote

HOW TO ARRANGE: *1.* Place a row of *kenzan* in the container, leaving spaces at both ends. *2.* Make bunches of about ten foxtails each, with the longer ones in back. *3.* Place five bunches of the foxtails to cover evenly about two thirds of the container from the left, and arrange the remaining in one bunch in the right side. *4.* Remove leaves from chrysanthemums and make them into three bunches. Insert one bunch between the foxtails and place the other two, side-by-side, in the left.

SUBSTITUTES: Colored pampas are even more effective than foxtails. *Flowers:* rose, carnation, narcissus.

90

When I visited Washington, D.C. at the time of the Cherry Blossom Festival, the beauty and magnificence of the blossoms were such that I forgot that I was from the land of the cherry blossoms. The endless clear sky, the pure hearts of the people I met there, the charm of the cherry blossoms and the river banks have grown deeper in my thoughts. This composition was arranged with hopes of another visit to that city.

MATERIALS: 11 red ilexes   O □ T

7 white ilexes   T

10 chrysanthemums   △

CONTAINER: a pair of earthenware vases

HOW TO ARRANGE: *1.* Fill the bottom of the containers with several *kenzan*. *2.* Arrange red ilexes in the front container, securing them firmly to the *kenzan*. Place the thick branches first, and spread out the branches like a fan. *3.* Place the white ilex in the back container. Slant one long stem toward the right so that its tip shows between the red branches. The remaining branches are slanted to the left. *4.* Make two bunches of chrysanthemums, one longer than the other. Place the shorter one in the front container, and the taller one in the rear container.

SUBSTITUTES: *Foliage:* spirea, cornus. *Flowers:* daffodil, tulip, orchid, gladiolus.

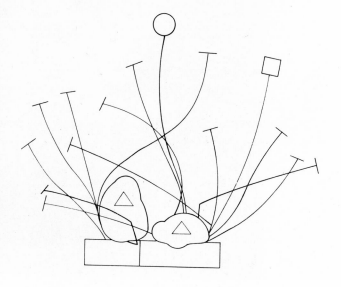

RECOLLECTION

This arrangement is an image of something beautiful and yet pathetic. A small composition in a spacious container is similar to a single recollection among various memories or an imagining of something nonexistent.

MATERIALS: 5 white camellias   ○ △ T
                     9 sprigs of young pine   □ T

CONTAINER: large emerald-colored basin

HOW TO ARRANGE: *1.* Placement of the *kenzan* will determine position of the arrangement. *2.* Remove leaves from the camellias, leaving only a few good ones near the flower. First place the longest stem to the far left, then add three others around the edge of the *kenzan*. *3.* Cut the longest pine to about one-half the length of the longest camellia; make the others shorter. Arrange pine around the three camellias. *4.* To complete the arrangement, add the last camellia to the right, outside the pine.

SUBSTITUTES: *Flowers:* lily, rose, chrysanthemum. *Foliage:* other species of pine, euonymus, nandin, enkianthus, spirea, cryptomeria, Japanese cypress.

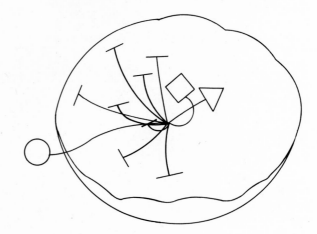

SPRING SONG

To hear the faint chirping of birds somewhere in the distance, when the air is still cold and your breath forms a mist, gives one the proud feeling of being secretly informed of the advent of spring. It even makes one feel like the creator of spring, and gives him the urge to spread the word around —no matter how faint the note may have been.

MATERIALS: 1 willow branch ○

            1 strelitzia □

            6 young pine stems △ T

CONTAINER: ceramic vase

HOW TO ARRANGE: *1.* Place a *kenzan* in the container; bend the willow branch and place it in the *kenzan*. *2.* Place the strelitzia at an angle facing the willow to form a balance of lines. *3.* Add five short pine stems to fill the base, and complete the arrangement by placing one longer pine stem slanted to the left.

SUBSTITUTES: *Foliage:* pussy willow, plum, forsythia, Japanese allspice (chimonanthus). *Flower:* lily, calla, anthurium. *Stems:* euonymus, asparagus fern.

96

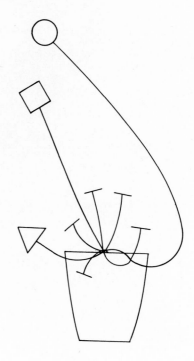

DAWN

Red and white colors and green bamboo are
closely related to New Year's. This arrangement
suggests a large rising sun painted on a hanging
scroll, a customary display during the New Year
season in Japan.

MATERIALS: 5 pussy willows ○ □ T
　　　　　　　2 camellias　　　　△ T

CONTAINER: a pair of handmade green bamboo
　　　　　　　　vessels

HOW TO ARRANGE: 1. This is *nage-ire* style and
no fixture is used. 2. Put the longest and
shortest willow branches in the front container.
Arrange other branches in the rear container.
3. The base of the stems must be cut in a slant
so that the cut end will stick firmly to the inner
wall of the container. 4. Remove leaves from
the camellias, leaving only those that add to the
rhythm of the flowers. The taller flower is placed
in the rear container, and the other is arranged
in the front container.

SUBSTITUTES: *Foliage:* spirea, broom. *Flowers:*
peony, lily, chrysanthemum.

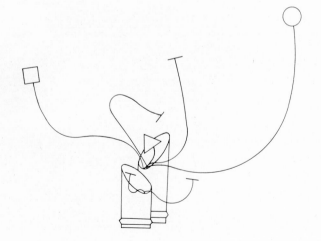

竹と針金

Non-seasonal Arrangements

There is no end to the eloquence of the improvisator, whose words flow so far and wide, sweetly, deeply, softly, tenderly, elegantly. He takes his audience to lands unknown, introduces them to strangers, and lets them hear music they have never heard before. And yet there is always something sad about him.

MATERIALS: 3 cypripedia ○ △ T
3 bleached asparagus ferns □
9 green wires

CONTAINER: glass vessel

HOW TO ARRANGE: *1.* Place orchids (cypripedia) in the right side of the container. Crush the stem of one cypripedium and place it bending down far to the right. *2.* Place asparagus stems in the container. Shape the sprays by curving the tips back toward the container. *3.* Following the lines of the flowers, arrange wires from the back of the flowers to the left and to the right. This addition of wires creates a motion of soft, low lines.

SUBSTITUTES: *Flowers:* Turkish bellflower, cattleya, strelitzia, iris, anthurium, rose, clematis. *Sprays:* babies' breath, gypsophila.

NOTE: Base your choice of flowers on the color of your container.

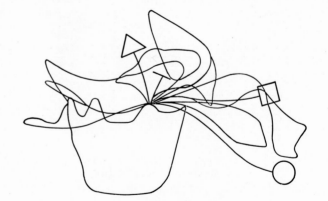

102

Chestnut-colored Hair

This arrangement symbolizes a beautiful young maiden with soft, chestnut-colored hair. On this fair-complexioned girl, any color of costume, rouge, or lipstick would be becoming. Sitting all alone in a spacious white-walled room, she seems to be absorbed in deep thought—probably dreaming of her future and picturing herself in womanhood.

MATERIALS: 8 ft. copper wire ◯

4 artificial flowers (anemone) △ T

CONTAINER: Venetian glass vase

HOW TO ARRANGE: *1.* Wind the wire on a pencil and make a coil. Then stretch it to the desired form; place it on the container. This spiral mass of wire also serves as a *kenzan*. *2.* Insert the flowers in the wire. Leaves are not used.

SUBSTITUTES: *Flowers:* rose, poppy, sweet pea, dahlia, anthurium, orchid.

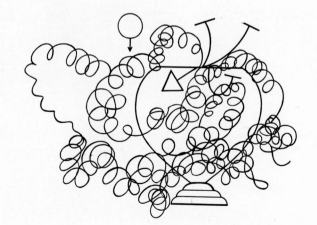

The Moon

The theme of this arrangement is the beautiful moon I saw in Venice, the birthplace of this container. The same moon shines over the whole world, but it is not appreciated in the same way everywhere. The degree of beauty depends upon its harmony with the location and landscape which surrounds the viewer. Does our planet call out to the moon, or is it that the moon longs for the human world?

MATERIALS: 4 ft. thin copper wire
　　　　　　7 buttercups

CONTAINER: Venetian glass vase

HOW TO ARRANGE: *1.* Make the wire spiral by winding it on a pencil. Then stretch it to form the desired shape, leaving some parts dense. *2.* Remove stems from buttercups, and glue flowers to the wire.

SUBSTITUTES: *Flowers:* any sprayed or painted flower or asparagus fern. If the arrangement is to be used for only a few hours, Japanese quince, cherry, or plum blossoms may be substituted.

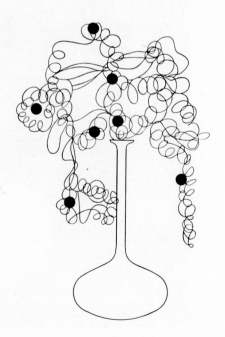

CONSTELLATION

When gazing at a constellation, it is easy to imagine colors such as those found in this arrangement. Sometimes the imagination adds shape to the colors, a dreamlike form which hangs hazy and suspended in the blackness of night.

MATERIALS: 2 plantains ○ □
5 cymbidiums △ T
6 ft. thin copper wire

CONTAINER: 2 emerald-colored vases

HOW TO ARRANGE: *1.* Place the longer plantain in the front container, and the shorter one in the rear (taller) container. *2.* Arrange cymbidiums at the base of the plantains. The flowers should be positioned at different levels in the respective containers to provide visual balance. *3.* To complete the arrangement, tie wires to each of the plantains.

SUBSTITUTES: *Stalks:* Japanese pampas, wheat, cattail. *Flowers:* narcissus, camellia, rose, gladiolus, sweet pea, freesia.

108

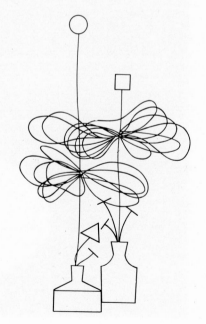

ROTATION

Japanese houses are, for the most part, made of plant materials, and flower arrangement must have developed as being the most compatible form of decoration for such houses. Ikebana also seems to merge well with our customs, temperament, and environment.

It is interesting to note that certain things of foreign origin, such as the mobile, have been adopted in Japan to create a beautiful and enchanting atmosphere. The mobile originated in the United States, but we find similar Japanese counterparts that have been utilized from long ago. The *furin*, or wind bell, is one of them. It gives a cool tinkling sound in the summer breeze. Another is the *yajirobe*, a toy that balances and moves on one's finger tip. These are gradually becoming familiar to Westerners.

The mobile shown here is made of bamboo

pieces softened by boiling with plume poppy. Hanging spiral beauty is created by the unity of circular shapes of threaded bamboo pieces and rounded brass strips.

MATERIALS: 2 camellias ◯ △

CONTAINER: handmade green bamboo vase

MOBILE: handmade with bamboo and brass

HOW TO ARRANGE: *1.* This is a *nage-ire* container, so bend the stems in order to hold them in place. *2.* Remove most of the leaves, allowing those near the flowers to remain. This trimming adds beauty both to the flowers and to the remaining leaves. Wipe leaves clean before placing the stems in the container.

SUBSTITUTES: *Flowers:* cherry, plum, Japanese quince (use one color of gay flowers), clematis, peony (two stems are sufficient to produce the form).

Basic Arrangements

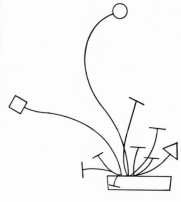

GROWTH

Moribana: Basic Upright Style

The pomegranates peeking through the green leaves resemble the flicker of candlelight, and express growth in their ripe red color. The yellow calla lilies add brightness and depth to the brilliant red.

MATERIALS: 2 pomegranate branches ○ □ T
4 calla lilies △ T

CONTAINER: porcelain bowl

HOW TO ARRANGE: The upright style (*risshin-kei*) is one of the two basic styles in ikebana and is applicable to both *moribana* and *nage-ire* arrangements. Repeated practice of this style and its variations listed on pages 121 and 122 will enable one to master all of the basic techniques in flower arrangement and to apply these to any freestyle composition. *1.* Cut the longest pomegranate branch to a length equivalent to:

(diameter + height of the container) × 1.5 (*see page 120*). Remove lower small branches, which are to be used later to cover the *kenzan*. Insert this branch in the *kenzan*, which is placed in the front left corner of the container, leaning to the left front at an angle of 10-15 degrees. *2.* Cut the second pomegranate branch to three-quarters the length of the first branch and remove leaves on the lower part. Place in *kenzan* at a 45-degree angle, again to the left front. *3.* Cut the first calla lily to one-half the length of the second pomegranate branch and place at a 75-degree angle to the right front. *4.* Cut the second, third, and fourth calla lilies short at slightly varying lengths and place them between the first calla lilly and the pomegranate branches. Complete the arrangement by placing three small pomegranate branches to cover the *kenzan*.

114

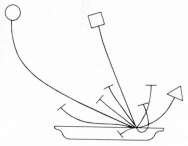

MIDNIGHT MOON

Moribana: Basic Slanting Style

Even in basic styles such as this arrangement, individual expression and imagery can be obtained through the proper selection of materials and their treatment. This composition is an image of a moonlight scene. It may be a corner in the garden, or in the stillness of a mountain pass.

MATERIALS: 6 forsythias (golden bell) ○ □ T
3 snapdragons △ T

CONTAINER: ceramic plate

HOW TO ARRANGE: The slanting style (*keishin-kei*) is one of the two basic styles in ikebana, and is used for both *moribana* and *nage-ire* arrangements. Repeated practice is required to master this basic style and its variations listed on pages 121 and 122 before one should attempt freestyle compositions. *1.* Cut the longest forsythia stem to a length one and one-half times that of the diameter plus the depth of the container (*see page 120*). Place this stem in the *kenzan* at the right rear of the container, slanting it at a 45-degree angle to the left front. Cut the second forsythia stem to about three-quarters the length of the first one and slant at an angle of 10-15 degrees to the left front. *2.* Cut the other forsythia stems short and place them to the front and back of the longest stem. *3.* Cut one snapdragon to three-quarters the length of the second forsythia and place in *kenzan* slanting to the right front at about 75-80 degrees. *4.* Place the remaining two snapdragons, one in front and the other in back, to fill the empty space at the base; this also helps to hide the *kenzan*.

SUBSTITUTES: *Foliage·* cherry, plum, magnolia, spirea, broom, Japanese quince. *Flowers:* stock, rose, chrysanthemum, gladiolus, narcissus, tulip.

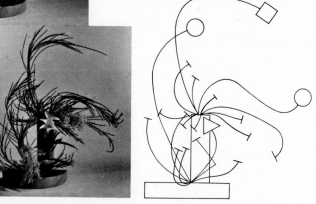

MOTHER AND DAUGHTER

Combination of Moribana and Nage-ire: Variation of Basic Style

This arrangement is a combination of *nage-ire* and *moribana* using two containers to create one arrangement. The characteristic feature of this style is in the drooping branches from the tall *nage-ire* container. Mother and daughter are very close and rely greatly on each other. The daughter is gay and colorful, while the mother shows dignity and stateliness.

MATERIALS: 10 Scotch brooms ○ □ T
　　　　　　6 acacias T
　　　　　　2 lilies △ T

CONTAINERS: set of ceramic *nage-ire* and *moribana* vessels (designed by Sofu Teshigawara)

HOW TO ARRANGE: Cut branches as specified on page 123. *1.* Place the longest drooping Scotch broom (○) in the tall container. Insert next stem (□) upright. Place another branch so that it hangs lower than the first. *2.* In the front container, place one long broom in the *kenzan* as the main stem. Then add one shorter assistant stem. *3.* Place three more shorter assistant stems in the tall container, and also two in the front container. *4.* Place acacias in the tall container first and then in the shallow one. Complete the arrangement by placing in the front container one lily as the main stem and one shorter lily as its assistant stem.

SUBSTITUTES: *Broom:* acacia, pussy willow, spirea, camellia, cercis. *Acacia:* gypsophila, asparagus fern, pampas grass.

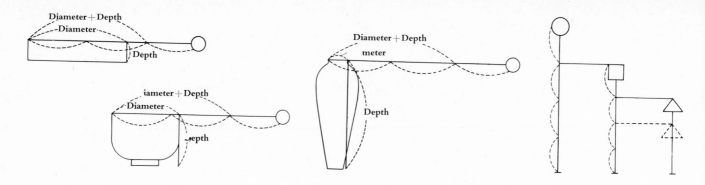

FUNDAMENTALS OF BASIC ARRANGEMENTS

You have been introduced to the Basic Upright Style (*page 114*), the Basic Slanting Style (*page 116*), and a combined Variation (*page 118*). These styles are applicable to both *moribana* and *nage-ire* arrangements. The standard BRANCH LENGTHS for these basic styles and BRANCH ANGLES for the basic styles and their variations are listed below. Repeated practice of these styles is necessary to acquire technique in dealing with various materials, and one is able to arrange freestyle compositions only after mastering these basic styles.

BRANCH LENGTHS

In traditional flower arrangement, the lengths and angles of the three main stems (*shin*, *soe*, and *hikae*) are basic in deciding the style of the arrangement. The beauty of an arrangement lies in the harmony created by the combination or balance of the plant material in conjunction with the container used for the composition. The fundamental measurements of the three main stems are always calculated in proportion to the size of the container. The following measurements are standard and the illustrations show the method of measurements:

○ First main stem (*shin*) = (diameter + height of the container) × 1.5

□ Second main stem (*soe*) = three quarters the length of the *shin*

△ Third main stem (*hikae*) = three-quarters or one-half the length of the *soe*

T Assistant stems (*jūshi*): should be shorter than each of the main stems they support. There is no limit in the number of assistant stems used in an arrangement.

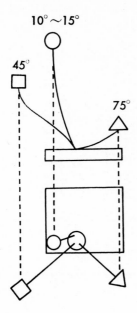

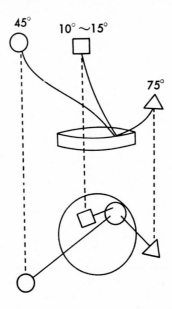

BRANCH ANGLES

Basic Upright Style

○ First main stem (*shin*):

place upright in the *kenzan* or *nage-ire* vessel tilted about 10-15 degrees to the left front.

□ Second main stem (*soe*):

tilted about 45 degrees to the left front.

△ Third main stem (*hikae*):

tilted about 75 degrees to the right front.

Basic Slanting Style

The difference between the upright and slanting styles is the reversed positions of the *shin* and *soe*. In the upright style, the *shin* is standing almost upright, but in the slanting style it is slanted to about 45-50 degrees.

○ First main stem (*shin*):

place tilted about 45 degrees to the left front.

□ Second main stem (*soe*):

place tilted about 10-15 degrees to the left front.

△ Third main stem (*hikae*):

place tilted about 75 degrees to the right front.

121

Basic Upright Style

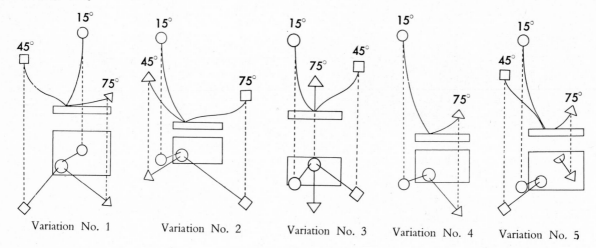

Variation No. 1   Variation No. 2   Variation No. 3   Variation No. 4   Variation No. 5

Basic Slanting Style

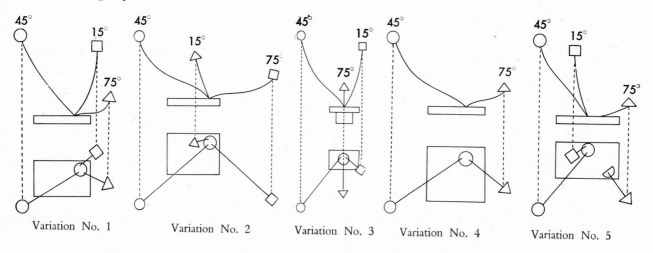

Variation No. 1   Variation No. 2   Variation No. 3   Variation No. 4   Variation No. 5

The above illustrations show the angles in the variations for each basic style (the *jūshi* is not used).

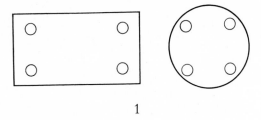

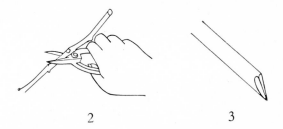

1

2

3

Freestyle arrangement, just as the word indicates, does not follow a set pattern. It permits free choice in the selection of materials, container, and composition, and also includes abstracts, which is a new development in the flower arrangement field. Individual expressions in line, shape, color, balance, and harmony are possible in the freestyle, but one must adhere to the basic principles as outlined in the basic styles. Therefore, satisfactory results are attainable in this freestyle arrangement only after careful study and repeated practice of the basic styles. The arrangements in this book are mostly freestyle compositions, which will serve as a guide to students who have mastered the basic styles.

Placement of Kenzan:

The general rule is that the *kenzan* is placed at either of the four corners of the container used for *moribana* arrangements (*illus. 1*). In some of the modern-shaped containers, however, the *kenzan* is placed in the center or, more likely, slightly off center.

TECHNIQUES

Cutting Branches

All branches, whether thin or thick, should be cut at a slant (*illus. 2*). Before cutting a branch, however, the most attractive side or angle of the branch must first be determined so that when placed in the *kenzan* or *nage-ire* container with the best side showing, the cut edge will face upward. Cutting in this manner makes it easier to place the branch in the *kenzan*, enables the the material to be held firmly at the desired angle, and also provides better resistance if the branch requires bending. In the case of *nage-ire*, the cut edge thus will lie flat and firmly against the inner surface of the containe .

When cutting a branch thicker than the size of your small finger, cut the branch at a slant once, then turn the branch around a little and make a second cut, like a pencil point (*illus. 3*).

Cutting Flower Stems

Flower stems should be cut straight across and placed at the desired angle in the *kenzan*.

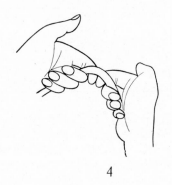

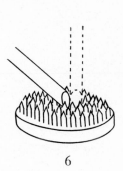

4 5 6

Preservation

To make arrangements last longer, always cut plants underwater (*mizu-giri*), since exposure to air prevents water from being absorbed through the stems. It most cases, withering plants regain freshness if cut underwater and kept in water for an hour or two. The use of a pump (*see page 126*) also helps to preserve summer plants.

Below is described additional treatment required by certain plants.

Japanese pampas grass and other similar plants: After cutting underwater, put the stem in a small bottle of vinegar or alcohol for a few minutes.

Clematis: Peel about one inch of the bark from the cut end.

Rose: Burn the cut end in a flame and cut underwater while still burning.

For woody materials, split the cut end into several parts to increase the area of water absorption.

Bending Branches

In bending branches thinner than your little finger, keep arms close to the body and hold stem with the forefingers of both hands touching each other (*illus. 4*). Bend slowly.

For branches thicker than your finger, make a slit on the outside surface (*illus. 5*) and bend slowly.

For flower stems, crush the stem by pressing with your fingers or bend by twisting gently.

Inserting Stems in the Kenzan

1. Grasp the stem with both hands at points about 1½ inches and 8 inches, respectively, from the cut end. Place the branch upright when securing in the *kenzan* and then give it a slant in the desired angle or direction (*illus. 6*).

2. To support very thin or weak stems, wrap tissue paper around the stem near the base, or wire another piece of stem, about one inch long, to

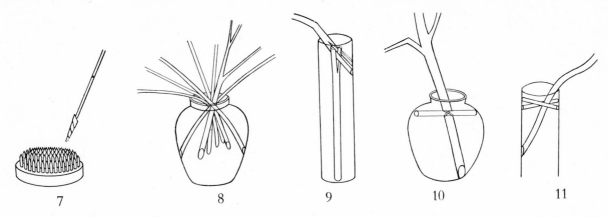

7   8   9   10   11

the base and then place the stem in the *kenzan* (*illus. 7*).

3. Flower stems should be placed at the desired angle when securing in the *kenzan*. The stem should be pressed into the *kenzan* with your fingers.

NOTE: Always remove all leaves up to about two inches from the cut end.

Securing Branches in Nage-ire Arrangements

Since a *kenzan* cannot be used in *nage-ire* containers, other devices or methods are required to hold the branches in place. The various fixtures listed below are for tall or bowl-shaped containers.

1. The simplest form is to bend the stems so that they rest against the mouth of the container (*illus. 8*).

2. The vertical fixture (*illus. 9*) is extremely helpful in securing branches at a desired angle in vases of almost any shape. The end of the branch should be split and interlocked with the split end of a discarded branch, slightly shorter than the height of the container.

3. The T-shaped fixture, which is made by tying a cross-bar to the branch, is used for rather shallow vases (*illus. 10*).

4. The X-shaped fixture is made by crossing two small twigs inside a cylindrical container about one inch down from its mouth. (*illus. 11*).

NOTE: Branches should be cut aslant even when these fixtures are used, so that the cut ends are flat and firm against the inside surface of the container.

Trimming

All bruised or torn leaves must be removed or trimmed. Branches that cross each other should be removed or bent away from other branches. All leaves inside the container, and branches that do not protrude from the container, should be removed.

125

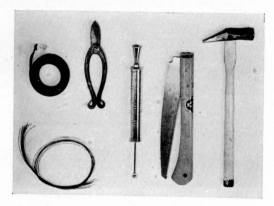

12   13

Necessary Equipment (*illus. 12*)

SHEARS:

The best policy is to buy a pair of good, sharp flower shears, even though they may cost a little more. Cheap blades are apt to chip off or get blunt easily. There are several kinds of shears, some with springs and others with loop handles. For cutting both thin and thick branches, the simplest and most convenient type is the one shown in the illustration.

WIRE:

Green florist wire is used for wiring stems and other materials.

TAPE:

Green tape is used to camouflage the wiring.

PUMP:

This pump is used to inject water or any other liquid into hollow stems (suck liquid into pump by pulling out handle and then insert nozzle in stem and push handle in), such as those of the lotus, yellow water lily, and other summer plants, in order to preserve them for a longer period of time. Another function of this pump is to spray water on finished arrangements. To facilitate pumping action, remove nozzle by unscrewing, then screw it onto the handle.

SAW:

A small saw with thin blades that fold into the handle is convenient for cutting thick branches. It is also easy to carry around.

HAMMER:

In large arrangements where materials are too big to use wire effectively, a hammer is necessary to nail the branches together. A small hammer as shown in the illustration will suffice.

15

16

KENZAN (needle-point holders):

The *kenzan* used in ikebana come in a wide variety of shapes and sizes (*illus. 13*). A good *kenzan* has fine and sharp needles and should be fairly heavy. The size and shape of the *kenzan* is decided by the container and flowers to be used in the arrangement. A pair of "sun-and-moon" *kenzan* (round and half-moon-shaped) is used most commonly and is extremely convenient. Flower stems are placed in the round *kenzan* and the half-moon one is used inverted (*illus. 14*), acting as a weight to give the arrangement

more stability. (Anchoring clay is used for this purpose in Western countries.) The half-moon *kenzan* is also used alone in small containers.

PEBBLES:

Pebbles are used to cover up and conceal the *kenzan* or in place of the *kenzan* when a transparent container is used for the arrangement (*illus. 13*).

AGATES:

These are also used to conceal the *kenzan* or in place of the *kenzan* when a transparent container is used (*illus. 13*).

CONTAINERS:

An assortment of containers is shown in the illustrations. The shallow, open containers are used for *moribana* (*illus. 15*) and the tall vases are used for *nage-ire* (*illus. 16*).

14

Glossary

hikae:	the third main stem or branch.
jushi:	branch or branches that support any of the three main branches.
kake-bana:	a wall arrangement.
kaki:	container in which flowers are arranged.
kenzan:	needle-point holders used to keep branches or flower stems in place.
mizu-age:	"water-raising"—a technique used to preserve cut flowers.
mizu-giri:	"water cutting"—cutting flower stems immersed in water.
moribana:	flower arrangement which uses a shallow container.
morimono:	arrangement using fruit, flowers, and vegetables.
nage-ire:	flower arrangement which uses a tall vessel.
shin:	the first main stem or branch.
soe:	the second main stem or branch.
suiban:	a rather large, shallow container.
uki-bana:	flower arrangement floated in water.